MW00831578

Teaching Tailwheel Flying

An Instructor's Toolkit

By

K. E. Bevier, CFII

Published by

The Walloon Press
Manning, South Carolina USA

ISBN 978-0-692-67350-8

Cover Photograph by Steven Richardson

Teaching Tailwheel Flying

An Instructor's Toolkit

TABLE OF CONTENTS

Dedication

This book is dedicated to the men of the Greatest Generation who had the most influence on my aviation career: Edward Bevier and Harold (Hal) Koenig.

Edward Bevier, my father, was a Private Pilot graduate of the Civilian Pilot Training Program in Ann Arbor, Michigan prior to World War II, and a radio operator with the 61stTroop Carrier Squadron throughout their European service between January, 1944 and August of 1945. His enthusiasm and romance with aviation infected me at an early age.

Hal Koenig was the chief flight instructor at Sumter County airport, near Shaw AFB in Sumter, SC, and a former P-51 Mustang pilot who survived two mid-air collisions in training, and a shoot-down on a strafing mission in France. After the war, Hal became an officer in the Air Force Reserve. He epitomized the very best qualities of a professional flight instructor and became the mentor I needed on my way to becoming an instructor myself.

I hope they both approve of this small effort.

Acknowledgements

Anyone who attempts to write as an expert in any field of aviation knows one little secret: there is always someone else, somewhere else, who knows more than themselves. To avoid the most egregious of misstatements and unwise advice, I have turned to Mr. John Pipkin and Mr. Stoney Truett, both long term and highly experienced professional pilots and instructors, to make sure my prose is at least understandable and my claims reasonable. Their help in reviewing this work has improved the product considerably.

In my chapter called Unusual Attitudes, I deal with some of the human factor aspects of flight training, specifically: anxiety and unrealistic expectations. To make sure I didn't lapse into some dialect of psychobabble and confuse more than illustrate, I asked for help from a professional, Dr. Daniel W. Lawther, PhD. His assistance has been invaluable in the preparation of this work because he himself is immersed in flight training for a pilot certificate. I would not have felt comfortable discussing the applied psychological aspects of flight training without his support and guidance.

Introduction

There are some seminal books about basic flying skills that have stood the test of time. Among them are *Stick and Rudder* by Rudolph Langweisch and *The Compleat Taildragger Pilot* by Harvey Plourde. Both cover virtually every aspect of stick-and-rudder and tailwheel flying except perhaps for some advanced techniques applicable to some of the specialized conditions encountered in the bush. They are both great books and I strongly recommend you find a place for them on your bookshelf.

Over twenty years ago I decided to specialize in tailwheel instruction, providing training and endorsements for already certificated pilots. Beginning with the FAA's creation of the Sport Pilot license I began to teach primary flight instruction for the Sport Pilot rating in addition to the tailwheel endorsement course, instrument work and other miscellaneous check-outs and flight reviews.

My experience with both ab-initio pilots and the already certificated, has convinced me the average CFI with a tailwheel endorsement in his logbook and modest amounts of tailwheel time, is pretty much a pioneer hiking into unknown territory when they begin to teach in tailwheel aircraft.

This book is not only for those instructors who wish to become better at teaching this tremendously important skill, but also for the pilots who want to know what they should be learning, and some of the techniques which may help them do so.

Prospective tailwheel pilots may also use this text as a blueprint for selecting an instructor and ensuring their training is thorough. It will also provide the vocabulary and concepts to communicate effectively during that process as well as some techniques appropriate to the student's particular learning style. The goal is maximizing knowledge transfer from the instructor while minimizing expensive training time.

The growth of the Sport Pilot certificate is giving new life to older tailwheel airplanes. I have watched prices steadily increasing over the past decade at rates well beyond inflation. The demand for tailwheel instruction will only increase in the years to come and as instructors, we must be prepared to teach the skills these new pilots need to fly safely. It is critical that foundational skills are rock solid, and learning to fly a tailwheel aircraft well, is one way to ensure that happens.

The Flight Instructor

Let me get this out of the way up front. If you don't enjoy teaching and showing others how to learn new skills, you will be better off doing something else with your time. It is unlikely you will excel at flight instructing if it doesn't please you in some way.

There are few things worse in aviation than a flight instructor who is fixated on building time for the next step in their goal of flying for the airlines, and who couldn't care less how effectively or quickly their students learn the required material. For them, students exist to allow the instructor to build hours.

This does not mean a good instructor will always feel overjoyed while lurching around the pattern on a steamy summer day with a student who believes the airplane will land itself when close to the runway. It does mean you need to recognize that the boring, done-it-a-million-times familiarity you feel as an instructor ranks a poor second behind your student learning how to fly.

Your primary objective as an instructor is to transfer a desired amount of your skill to the student. If you cannot give your student your best work, in flight or on the ground, you are failing them and betraying the trust they have placed in you.

I know that sounds harsh, and it is. But no matter how I think about the process it always comes down to you as an instructor giving your best, 100% of the time. Anything less is unacceptable.

Instead of resting on your current skills, you must be willing to work at becoming an expert. You must be able to admit to yourself there might be a better way to help poor Dan understand how to flare into a three-point as the aircraft settles from the round-out. You must focus every bit of your intellect and ability on the business at hand, thinking about what might work better for each and every student you have. If you cannot learn to place your student's interests first, you will never become a true professional.

Everyone learns differently and at a different pace. You must know when and how to deviate from the lesson plan. Low ceilings might preclude a lesson on minimum controllable airspeed but still allow learning pattern entries. Perhaps a pitch control exercise well above minimum controllable airspeed and at reduced power might be substituted instead. Do you really think the sixty year old who can fly once every two weeks will learn as quickly as a twenty-year old student who can fly every day? You must have the ability to be flexible in your instruction, and design a lesson plan for that student for that particular flight based on their current needs. To be effective, you must engage on a personal level with your student to get a better idea of their educational background, life experience and motivation in order to create effective training techniques.

My advice is to develop your own generic lesson plans based on the must-have skills in the Practical Test Standards (PTS) and Federal Aviation Regulations (FARs), and ensure your students are taught to the standards expected in every one of them. How you break down the required skills and sequence the teaching of the components of those skills into a series of lessons is one of the bigger challenges for a flight instructor.

You must be able to change teaching technique ad hoc, to create a new exercise out of thin air, while flying in same, to solve your student's current hang-up. Instruction must never be simply keeping them safe until, with enough repetition, they accidentally discover how to perform the maneuver. You must be pro-active with a student's training at all times, constantly seeking ways to improve their skill levels in all maneuvers. To do less is a disservice to the student.

Most students will learn, to one degree or another, from aural, visual and kinesthetic inputs. The challenge to a flight instructor is finding which method or combination of methods, works best for that student for the subject being taught. The reality is that most students will learn different subjects with different degrees of success depending on the approach chosen.

Some students will respond to an explanation of why the tailwheel should be pinned to the ground during takeoff until there is sufficient airflow over the rudder to maintain directional control. Some will respond to "Keep the stick back until the Airspeed Indicator begins to flicker." Others will need the experience of lifting the tailwheel too early in a stiff left crosswind to understand.

Being a flight instructor can be pretty boring at times. How many bounced landings have you witnessed while lightly grasping the control stick, hoping your student will do the right thing? But the payoff is when they finally recover gracefully after the umpteenth bounced landing because they remembered to hold the stick back. You hope it wasn't a fluke as you slow to a stop, check the trim and carb heat and launch again, and again, and . . .

But this is the job, ladies and gentlemen: not much glory, sometimes long and inconvenient hours, sometimes-marginal weather, and sometimes-marginal aircraft. If you work hard at bringing your best game to your students in these conditions, you will, in time, become a successful, respected and professional flight instructor.

And no, you won't be perfect 100% of the time. Sometimes you'll feel like snapping at a student because you haven't had anything to eat for breakfast, it's pushing mid-afternoon, and you've just explained short-field takeoff technique for the seventeenth time. Your oh-so-witty put down will not help, nor will a loud sigh over the intercom. What will help, is to challenge yourself instead. Ask: *What have I not told or shown this student in order to correct their problem?* It is certainly good practice to ask the student what they themselves think the problem is, and to listen carefully to their response. They may provide you some insight you can use to correct the situation or they may not. But regardless of the utility of their response, you will have pro-actively engaged them in the learning process, a critical step in developing open and free flowing communications.

My point here is that all students are different, and it is up to you to find the best way to teach them. Unlike classroom instruction in a lecture format, one size does not fit all. This is the ultimate challenge for an instructor, adapting your teaching style to best serve each student and, contrary to the opinions of some non-instructors, this is a challenging and daunting task requiring a lot of brain time, constant close observation, creative solutions and the patience of a saint.

The FAA provides an invaluable publication that provides an excellent background on learning theory, psychological aspects of personality and how some personality traits may affect learning. I strongly suggest you download a copy of the Aviation Instructor's Handbook (FAA-H-8083-9) and refresh your memory on the subject matter areas covered in this excellent work.

Training Aircraft

One of the enduring debates among pilots who fly old tailwheel aircraft is which is the better airplane: the Piper Cub or the Aeronca Champ. The question should really be which is the better training aircraft for the student pilot? Which airplane will provide the best service in learning stick and rudder skills? In my opinion, both will do an excellent job in teaching stick and rudder skills. Each of these aircraft is a safe airplane to fly but a difficult airplane to fly well; exactly the characteristics you want in a trainer for the student pilot to deal with.

When it comes to maintenance cost, ease of entry, visibility and access to the engine controls, the Champ is clearly the better choice, and I would challenge any Cub owner in the country to attempt to convince me the Cub's standard brakes and bungeed landing gear are better from a maintenance cost and reliability point of view. But I love the Cub, for all its drawbacks, just as much as I love the Champ. Both are tremendously good choices for learning tailwheel flying. My preference as an instructor and owner/operator is more clear-cut.

Sitting up front in the Cub with the student behind you, removes your ability to see what your student is looking at. Are they chasing the airspeed indicator? Are they focusing down the runway during their round-out? Are they picking up a height reference by glancing off at a slight angle towards the edge of the runway? As an instructor, that information is important, and removing the student from view reduces your ability to identify a problem and formulate a solution. For this reason, as well as ease of entry to the back seat, all round visibility, easier access to all engine controls and a much easier to use trim system, I prefer the Champ, which I consider to be the best primary trainer ever built. There are some other fine flying aircraft from both the WW2 era as well as post-war and even some of the SLSA offerings, but they are not designed to handle the abuse and hard use that training aircraft receive. The Aeronca 7AC Champ is simply outstanding in this role.

There is one advantage to training in a Cub: there is no forward visibility for students and they are forced to develop directional control by using their peripheral vision. Zero forward visibility is common among many tailwheel aircraft, and directional control under these conditions is an important skill to master. All is not lost in the Champ, however. If you put the student in the back seat for a few hours of landing practice near the end of their training, the same skill as in the Cub can be easily learned.

The only real difference between a three-point landing in a tailwheel aircraft and a landing in a tricycle gear airplane is a slightly higher pitch attitude in the tailwheel aircraft. All landing loads should be absorbed by the main-gear in a tricycle gear aircraft and *none* by the nose-gear. Sadly, the number of three-pointers and wheel-barrowed landings I see in tricycle gear aircraft seems to be on the rise; a direct result of the pilot not learning to pitch the nose up into a slightly shallower three-point attitude than is used in a tailwheel aircraft. When the nose-wheel is abused with landing loads, the gear itself can be damaged, as well as bending the firewall, an expensive repair in most cases.

Learning proper landing technique in a tail-wheel aircraft can pay huge benefits to pilots who subsequently transition into tricycle gear airplanes. It is so important, I first teach my Private Pilot candidates to fly the Champ before transitioning them into a tricycle gear airplane for their night and instrument work.

Instructor Tailwheel Experience

The amount of experience you should have before you begin to give tailwheel instruction depends as much on your ability to fly the training aircraft, as it does on your skill as a teacher. As an instructor you must recognize the mistakes your student is making in controlling the aircraft and then formulate methods for them to correct that behavior. This requires an intimacy with the training aircraft and how it behaves to the various control inputs and external forces acting upon it. This intimacy only happens with long experience in a multitude of weather, wind, and runway conditions. You must be expert in how the wind, density altitude, loading, runway surface and slope affect performance. You should be fully capable of flying the airplane routinely and competently to the very edges of the performance envelope for two very important reasons.

First, you must allow your student to make mistakes. It is the only way for them to learn. You must be able to know when to intervene, and you will only know that if you are intimate with the airplane. You must wear the airplane like a comfortable set of clothes. Obviously this type of competency comes not just from hours spend sucking avgas through the carburetor on sight-seeing flights, but from concentrated practice and training designed to push the aircraft to the edges of its capability. This degree of expertise does not develop overnight.

The second reason is you must demonstrate MCA and stalls to your students in order to teach them where the limits of performance are. Let me go on record by saying I disagree with the FAA position that advocates the teaching of *stall recognition* vs actual *stall recovery*. Most of what passes today as stall recognition is when the stall horn goes off in a Cessna 152 or, even worse, in a Cessna 172 being used for primary instruction. The stall horn in these aircraft is actually set to go off approximately 5-10 knots above an actual stall. This approach will only teach the student horn recognition, not stall recognition. What will happen to them should they fly an aircraft without a stall-warning device and find themselves approaching an impending stall which they've never been trained to recognize? What if the stall-warning device is defective?

You must be able to teach your students to ride the feathery edge of a stall straight ahead and in turns, and to acquire the feel required to recognize, and fly at, minimum controllable airspeed, defined by the FAA as "a *speed* (italics are mine) at which any further increase in angle of attack or load factor, or reduction in power will cause an immediate stall."[1] The FAA further comments, "a feel for the airplane at very low airspeeds must be

---

[1] "Airplane Flying Handbook." FAA.gov. Accessed October 30, 2015. http://www.faa.gov/regulations_policies/handbooks_manuals/aircraft/airplane_handbook/ , 4-1.

10

developed to avoid inadvertent stalls and to operate the airplane with precision."[2]

I would re-write the definition of MCA to say: An *angle of attack* at which any further increase in angle of attack, angle of bank, or reduction in power will cause an immediate stall. This more clearly states that a wing stall is a function of the wing's angle of attack and the load it supports, and not the aircraft's airspeed parallel to its longitudinal axis.

Another area of expertise I would stress is your mastery of crosswind technique for both three-point and wheel-landings. You should be able to demonstrate these landings to the maximum ability of the aircraft. Furthermore, you should be able to demonstrate alternate techniques that may work in the aircraft you are teaching in. For example, a powered three-point is a superb squirrely crosswind technique in the Champ as well as in many other tailwheel aircraft.

It should be obvious by now that I think you should have mastery of the airplane you teach in. If you do not, or feel uncomfortable demonstrating all required maneuvers to a student, log some concentrated flight time in preparation. There are no short cuts here. If you are unable to comfortably fly the aircraft to the limits of its capability, you will have trouble letting your students learn some valuable lessons from their mistakes.

---

[2] Ibid.

Common Tailwheel Training Problems

The issues I'll talk about in detail all involve control of the aircraft during either takeoff or landing. I teach how to unlock the tailwheel for sharp taxi turns when necessary, and also how to position the controls to hold the airplane down in high winds, but nobody seems to have a real problem in learning how to do these things. Both can be amply explained, demonstrated and practiced at most airports.

The problems that plague students the most are all associated with either the takeoff or landing of the aircraft: directional control, not lifting tail enough during takeoff, performing the round-out for three-point landings, performing the flare for three-point landings, judging downward velocity during a wheel landing, bringing stick forward during wheel landings, getting the tailwheel on the ground during a wheel landing, retaining crosswind corrections after touchdown until aircraft has stopped, and bounced landing recovery from both wheel and three point landings.

I'll talk about each of these issues at length in subsequent short chapters with some suggestions to help your students learn the required skills. But I would like to point out that students who bring the greatest amount of fine pitch control to the task of flying tailwheel aircraft have an advantage. I've noticed over the years that helicopter, glider and instrument rated pilots have learned the type of fine pitch control required for wheel landings. As a bonus, the glider and helicopter pilot have been using their feet for yaw control since learning to fly, a situation that is sadly not true for many of the fixed wing pilots trained in tricycle gear aircraft. This may not sound like a big deal, but rudder input to keep the fuselage of a tailwheel aircraft aligned with the runway during a landing is critical and rudder input must become automatic for the pilot: there is no time to think about it during a landing.

I know there are instructors who will argue vehemently that your feet can learn to fly in a tricycle gear airplane just as well. I'm sure there are a few pilots out there for whom this is true; it's just that in my twenty-plus years as an active flight instructor I've never met one. I care about the lack of footwork I see in the students who come to me for a tailwheel endorsement and who must learn to recognize, and act upon, the slightest change in yaw if necessary. I strongly believe that one's first exposure to flying fixed wing aircraft should be in gliders or tailwheel aircraft. The modern tricycle-gear airplane robs the student of the ability to learn proper rudder usage for every phase of training except the right rudder required at high power and high angles of attack during takeoffs, steep climbs and power-on stalls.

To summarize, the most egregious lack of control issues for tailwheel students, seem to come from lack of yaw control and fine pitch control of the aircraft. If a student's flying has included copious amounts of experience in either or both of these skills, their training will generally go fairly quickly.

The following chapters deal with the list of specific issues mentioned above, along with some ideas I've used to help students acquire competency in performing them. Please keep in mind that your criteria for when the student has learned the skill is not performance to some sliding standard you might have based upon your own skills. The criteria should always be: is the student capable of both performing this maneuver to realistic standards, and safely recovering from a failed attempt. If those two criteria are met in your teaching of the student, they will have the skills to improve their flying by further solo practice.

Directional Control

I'm addressing directional control first because it is absolutely fundamental to flying a tailwheel airplane. It was the first skill taught to aviation cadets in France during the First World War. Perhaps it would be more accurate to state it was the first skill *learned* by students rather than *taught* to students.

Instructors were in such short supply in France that the job of learning directional control was placed squarely on the student by creating flightless training aircraft and having the student learn to taxi back and forth across a mile long open field; at first slowly, then fast enough to lift the tail into a high speed two-point taxi and then lower it back to the ground again during deceleration. These aircraft were called *penguins,* and were high wing monoplanes equipped with very wide landing gear, clipped wings and a low-powered engine. It took most students several weeks to teach themselves how to taxi in a straight line and avoid ground loops and roll overs. I've never been able to find any statistics on the numbers of trainees killed or injured during this process but undoubtedly the method served its primary purpose of protecting the scarce number of instructors in existence at that time.

Today, adequate control of the aircraft can be taught in several sessions of high-speed taxi maneuvers, exactly the same way as the students of the First World War learned with one exception. You'll be using a flyable aircraft and *you* will be in the aircraft during the process, keeping them out of trouble and suggesting corrective actions like using quick jabs at the rudders to stop the undesired yaw rather than pushing and holding the pedal down.

Obviously, you must be absolutely comfortable in recovering the mistakes of your student. This means instantly assessing whether or not you must over-ride their rudder or stick movements and acting accordingly. With some strong-legged students, this can be a high anxiety experience. A prior briefing about them letting go of the controls quickly when you start screaming into the intercom, or frantically tapping them on the shoulder, is advised.

The number one problem here is the student being "behind the aircraft" and not recognizing that momentum will determine the airplane's near-future attitude. It takes a finite amount of time for the rudder to deflect air and yaw the airplane in a specific direction. When the student presses the left rudder to correct a yaw to the right, they don't realize it takes a moment for the aircraft to begin to respond to their input, and that the response rate varies with the airspeed. Since the nose doesn't move instantly, they press harder, adding even more of a yawing force. But now the rudder begins to bite, delivers more yaw then intended and the nose of the aircraft suddenly points sharply to one side of the centerline. This, in turn, provokes a huge opposite-rudder input and you are suddenly off to the races towards the side of the runway. My advice during this training is to simply jab at the pedals and get off. Then jab more frequently and harder if you don't get the required result. This generally keeps them from holding a pedal down and over correcting until the airplane is yawing even more in the opposite direction.

To help the student learn, start with three point taxi exercises. Line up on the centerline and taxi down the runway in three-point attitude, stick hard back. Guard the stick against extreme forward movement, and you yourself control the throttle. Begin slowly and do not increase speed significantly until the student can successfully keep the aircraft within a gear width of the centerline for the entire distance. Repeat at successively higher speeds until you've reached the speed where the tail should be lifted to avoid a three-point lift-off. In the Champ or the Cub, a good speed to use is when the airspeed needle starts to quiver. When the student is competent in controlling the aircraft under these conditions, it is time to introduce lifting the tail. It is appropriate to discuss gyroscopic precession of the propeller at this time and the strong effect it can have in yawing the aircraft to the left (for a clockwise engine rotation as seen by the pilot) when the tail is lifted, *and to the right when the tail is suddenly lowered.*

Now have the student bring the aircraft into a level pitch attitude by using forward stick when the airspeed begins to quiver, but suggest they control the speed the tail comes up over a three second period as this will reduce the degree of swerve to the left. Tell them the faster the tail lifts, the more pronounced will be the swerve. Caution them that if they go forward and then jerk back, the aircraft can swerve to the right as well.

In an attempt to avoid the left-turning swerve, students are reluctant to lift the tail sufficiently to put most of the aircraft weight on the main gear out of fear of a prop strike. It is essential they learn to do so or gusty crosswinds will dribble them sideways across the runway while attempting to lift off in three-point attitude. Let them know if they avoid touching the brakes while lifting the tail, it is virtually impossible to get a prop strike. This is because, as the horizontal stabilizer rises at an angle to the relative wind, the air-loads will eventually overpower the ability of the elevators to lift the tail further and force the prop into the dirt. A demonstration of this may be in order in cases of severe disbelief. Nevertheless, most students are reluctant to go fully forward with the stick and wait for the tail to lift. Instead, when the nose starts to pitch down, they jerk the stick back, thus inducing a swerve to the right. Some will saw the stick forward and back yielding a strange combination of forces on the CG of the airplane as it darts back and forth across the runway; it feels something like I imagine being in a paint shaker would feel like.

18

Help the student by getting on the controls with them and placing the aircraft into a two point, high-speed taxi. Remember you will need to retard the throttle to keep the airspeed at a comfortable margin below lift off. In a Champ or Cub forty to fifty miles per hour seems to work fine.

Now comes the fun part. While keeping an eye on the amount of available runway in front of you, reduce the throttle gradually to idle while telling your student to hold the tail up as long as possible. When they can no longer do so, or feel they are losing directional control, have them smoothly pull the stick aft and pin the tailwheel to the runway again. This usually yields some pretty wild gyrations the first few attempts, so stay on top of their control inputs with a hand on the stick and your feet ready to apply differential braking. In the worst of cases it may take some rudder deflection and a burst of power to remedy the situation, especially in a strong crosswind. Remember what I said about being expert in the airplane? This is one of the reasons why. If you don't feel comfortable in your ability to recover a student's errors while doing this exercise, then you deny them the ability to quickly learn a critical skill.

The last step of course, is having them manage the throttle. This usually results in a deterioration of directional control for a few attempts before the student is able to integrate this last task into their rudder and stick control.

When the student is able, like his First World War counterpart, to taxi up and down the runway, lifting the tail and bringing it back down again at will with coordinated use of power, you have taught them directional control in a tailwheel airplane. When they have mastered this skill, their takeoffs will become a lot less exciting. Gone will be the overwhelming need to jerk the airplane into the air before mowing down some runway lights and unless you are addicted to adrenaline, this is a positive development.

I like to spend about half of the first, second and third lessons, if necessary, devoted to this exercise, while using the other lesson time to teach other aspects of flight. For primary students, straight and level, turn coordination, minimum controllable airspeed and stalls must be taught from scratch. For tailwheel endorsement students, their skills must be transferred into the tailwheel aircraft and demonstrated to your satisfaction.

Although you might like to say you have taught the student directional control, keep in mind that the procedure above is taught during acceleration to flying speed. Sad to say, the skill does not always transfer to the landing phase of flight.

I will cover crosswind correction in another section because of its importance. What I'm referring to here is not keeping the longitudinal axis of the airplane parallel to the centerline of the runway during touchdown.

Most students that have trained in tricycle gear aircraft as well as the ab-initio students seem to believe somewhere deep inside that if they can get the airplane down close to the runway in ground effect, their job is over and the aircraft will land itself. I have no explanation why they might think this is the case other than, in the case of new pilots, they simply haven't been told and, in the case of already certificated pilots, they have become sloppy with runway alignment after flying much more forgiving tricycle gear aircraft.

Whatever the reason, your student must be disabused of this desire to let the airplane land itself unless of course you want to teach ground-loops, wingtip damage, and landing gear demolition. Generally a reminder or two about holding them responsible for the insurance deductible does the trick. You must teach them to actively fly the aircraft, including control positioning in high winds, until it has come to a complete stop, the engine is not running and you are ready to get out and put it in the hangar. In the chapter on teaching the flare, I will discuss an exercise that will help correct a student's propensity to believe your aircraft has an Auto-land feature.

Pitch Control

Pitch control and, in the case of tailwheel aircraft, fine pitch control, is an absolute necessity. Lack of this skill will cause the student to lift the nose too high during either the round-out or flare of a three-point landing, causing them to drop the airplane onto the runway from a potentially damaging altitude; or not lift it enough, causing the main gear to bang on the runway first, initiating the first of multiple crow-hops down the runway, perhaps turning the landing into a pilot induced oscillation and a prop strike. Lack of fine pitch control can also case an erratic descent rate towards the runway during a wheel landing as the student saws the stick forward and aft, and is the culprit behind a bounced landing and attempts by the student to force the nose down onto the runway, giving the prop the opportunity to shred its tips on the pavement (I strongly recommend using wooden props to protect the engine against sudden stoppage).

Pitch control is easily evaluated by observing how close your student can hold airspeed during a turning descent, like in the pattern, or on a long final approach where the aiming point should remain static in the windshield.

For the first few hours of training it is a good idea to cover the airspeed indicator in order to force the student's vision outside to the horizon. This will help you to directly evaluate their pitch control—or lack thereof. Teach them the pitch attitudes and power settings for full-power climb, cruise, cruise descent and flying in the pattern. Occasionally, have them lift the cover on the airspeed indicator to see how close they can come without having an instrument to reference. This, more than anything you can say, will convince them to use the airspeed indicator only as a supporting instrument. A safety bonus is your student is now keeping their eyes outside the cockpit, watching the horizon and looking for other aircraft.

One exercise you can use to improve a students pitch control is, ironically, based upon use of the airspeed indicator. Find some of those large sticky-paper peel-off colored dots at your business supply store. During flight at pattern airspeed (I use 60 in the Champ), have the student stick the dot (an alternative is drawing a dot with a dry-erase pen) on his horizon on the windshield (while you fly the airplane). Now have the student release their usual death grip on the stick, grasping it only with thumb and index finger, and fly precisely at sixty by keeping their dot on the horizon. The airspeed indicator should be covered. When they are able to mostly keep their dot on the horizon, uncover the airspeed and let them see how well the horizon reference works. Now have them smoothly pitch up over a slow count of five and bring the aircraft to 55, hold for a count of five, followed by the same slow count while pitching back down to 60, hold, and then down again to 65. Point out to the student that if they remember the position of the dot above and below the horizon, they can smoothly adjust to the desired airspeed by visual reference. Also point out they could use the angular distance to the top of the cowling as a reference by keeping the angle constant. Show them how the airspeed indicator lags several seconds behind by having them pitch up smoothly from 65 to 55 and note how long the instrument takes to reflect that change.

Use the dot for at least two training sessions and then remove it from the windshield. By keeping the airspeed indicator covered during this transition, the student quickly transfers their reference from the now missing dot to the top of the cowling. If they continue to have trouble with pitch and power settings, repeat the dot exercises until the process clicks into place for them. This is a skill that must be acquired before the student begins either three-point or wheel landings, and is critical to airspeed control in the pattern. The student's transition to the correct pitch attitude for the various power settings described above should become automatic as well as their ability to hold a consistent airspeed during both straight and level, gliding and turning flight.

Crosswind Correction

This topic seems to foment a lot of discussion among pilots. The rhetoric is usually centered on the best way to correct for crosswinds during landing: crab or sideslip. I don't think I have ever heard an argument about the best way of taking off in a crosswind. But here as well, there are two distinct schools of thought: slip it into the air then crab into the wind to maintain alignment, or try to keep it straight with opposite rudder until you can jerk it into the air and into a crab. Let us talk about takeoffs first as this will inform to a great extent the considerations necessary for the use of different landing techniques.

Imagine if you will, a ninety-degree crosswind from the left at the maximum crosswind the combination of pilot and aircraft can handle. With the aircraft sitting still on the runway, the wind is attempting to lift the upwind wing while simultaneously turning the aircraft's nose directly into the wind. Without brakes on the main gear, the tailwheel may or may not have enough friction on the ground to prevent the airplane from weathervaning 90 degrees to the runway centerline. With differential braking of the main gear, the pilot is able to exert enough friction on the main gear tires to prevent the aircraft from yawing into the wind.

However, as soon as the brakes are released to begin the ground-roll, the yawing effect of the wind must be counteracted with the only yaw control available, the rudder. The wind is still trying to lift the upwind wing however and, as soon as the upwind wheel comes off the ground, the aircraft will yaw viciously into the wind. When this happens, the student will jam downwind rudder in an attempt to yaw the airplane back into alignment but neglect to lower the wing. This action causes the aircraft to yaw downwind, but also causes it to roll in the same direction, which creates a further lifting of the upwind wing. The wing may lift to the point where the opposite wing tip can strike the runway, causing a vicious yaw to downwind and, if the student has not brought the stick fully aft, the aircraft may go over on its back.

If not yet to rotation speed, total power reduction and simultaneous application of all three controls is necessary to prevent that scenario from happening: full stick deflection into the wind to lower the wing, full back stick deflection to get (or keep) the tailwheel on the ground, and full rudder deflection to align the aircraft to the runway. Once all three wheels are again on the ground, judicious braking can be applied to prevent a runway excursion.

If close to rotation speed and at full power you have only seconds to decide what to do. In any case, you must immediately lower the upwind wing and apply enough rudder to prevent a runway excursion. Once you are again lined up with the runway, you can decide whether or not to abort the takeoff by chopping power and getting the tail-wheel back on the ground. However, if you come back with the stick too suddenly at close to rotation speed, you can balloon into the air, which may or may not work out for you depending on your subsequent actions.

If you have not gotten the aircraft under control at this point, it is probably best to come back and into the wind with the stick while the aircraft weathervanes into the wind, and then apply as much brake as you can without skidding the tires. You might take out a few runway lights and ding up your landing gear, but whatever you strike will be at a fairly low speed, causing minimal damage to the aircraft and protecting the occupants.

Now, replay the same takeoff scenario, but at the beginning of the ground roll hold the stick hard into the wind, which will cause the aileron to push the wing down, keeping it from lifting during takeoff. Everything looks good, we're accelerating down the runway, the airplane is getting light on its feet and suddenly, it starts start skittering sideways. Novice pilots will attempt to jerk the airplane into a climb before they take out some runway lights and, if Mother Nature is kind to them that day, they will have enough airspeed to do so. If not, then taking out a few runway lights will probably be the least of their worries.

The big problem here is not enough weight on the main gear to prevent the wind from pushing the aircraft sideways across the runway. The correction is simple: lift the tail higher than normal so the wing is at a negative angle of attack until you rotate and begin your climb-out. This technique, combined with holding the upwind wing down, will put most of the weight of the aircraft on the upwind landing gear. At lift-off, your downwind wing will lift first then the upwind wing as you begin your climb-out in a sideslip. When you are sure of a positive rate of climb, simply crab into the wind, level your wings to get rid of the drag being caused by the cross-controlled slip, and climb to altitude.

Let me point out that with this takeoff technique, the aircraft is always aligned to the runway centerline by holding the upwind wing down, opposite rudder is applied in order to track the centerline, the downwind wheel lifts first and the aircraft begins climbing in a side-slip. What if we simply reversed this procedure in order to land: sideslip for alignment, upwind wheel(s) touch down first and as we slow down, the downwind main-gear wheel follows?

Of course, if we are landing three-point in a full stall with the upwind wing lowered into the wind, the upwind main-gear wheel and tailwheel will touch at the same time. With power off, the aircraft will quickly decelerate through the speed where there is not enough weight on the main gear to prevent the aircraft from being pushed sideways across the runway. The pilot will need to increase the amount of aileron and rudder deflection to maintain alignment as the aircraft slows and the control surfaces become less effective.

Before we talk about other techniques used in crosswind landings, let us quickly review the nature of our adversary: the wind. However fast it is blowing on the surface, the wind velocity increases with altitude because of ground surface friction. For a 10-knot direct crosswind on the runway surface, we may have 20 knots just fifty feet above the runway. When we begin our final approach at a few hundred feet AGL, we may discover we do not have enough rudder effectiveness to keep the aircraft aligned with the runway when using a side-slip, and we must resort to crabbing into the wind as well as side-slipping to keep the CG of the aircraft over the centerline. As we descend, the wind-speed may decrease enough to allow us to again align the aircraft, at which point we land as described above. But what if we are still crabbing into the wind as we approach the runway surface? It could be disastrous to touch down crabbed into the wind; we would instantly ground loop and probably put the airplane on it's back after ripping off a wingtip.

The answer to this dilemma is what brings us to the origin of one of the major crosswind landing techniques. The procedure is to quickly yaw the aircraft into alignment while lowering the wing into the crosswind as you settle towards the runway. A bit of power can be used to help the nose around and provide a bit more rudder control authority. The main gear will hopefully touch down before the aircraft begins to drift sideways. Full stick back and into the wind is then used to keep the upwind main gear and tailwheel on the ground. Some downwind brake (if gear is on runway) and simultaneous throttle may be needed to maintain alignment as the aircraft slows. (Note that for gliders and transport category aircraft with large wingspans, one must dispense with lowering the wingtip.)

Obviously this latter technique requires a high degree of skill to perform successfully, but is used by bush pilots everywhere in extreme crosswinds, and actually permits operations in higher winds than can be safely handled with the pure side-slip technique. For the rest of us mortals, it is much safer to stick to the pure sideslip technique when near the runway. If we run out of rudder, abort the landing and find a friendlier place to land.

This sideslip technique is the method most favored today in flight schools. Students are taught to roll the wing down into the wind when turning final and align the aircraft to the runway centerline with opposite rudder. The aircraft is then flown down to the runway surface, while adjusting the amount of wing down and opposite rudder to maintain alignment. A variation on this technique at some schools is to crab during the first part of the final approach then shift into the sideslip method as the aircraft approaches the runway.

It is impossible to claim there is one technique better than others all the time, in all aircraft, for all pilots. However, the simplest techniques

30

should be taught to new tailwheel students in order to provide them a proven, safe method of flying in crosswinds. I teach the conventional sideslip technique until the student is competent, and then have them try using a crab during the first two-thirds of the approach before converting to the sideslip so they understand this variation as well.

I like to start training students in cross wind techniques by finding a long section of straight road in the practice area that is as perpendicular to the prevailing wind as possible. Start at a thousand feet AGL, reduce power and airspeed to pattern settings. Have the student keep the center of the aircraft over the road with the wings level. They will quickly see they have to crab in one direction or another to do so. Advise them this is exactly the same as the crosswind correction used to fly a course over or parallel to the road. Also point out that they are maintaining their altitude with the current power setting.

Now, show them how to lower a wing into the wind and line the axis of the aircraft up with the road while telling them this is how you keep the airplane aligned to a runway when landing. Point out that slips of any kind are cross-controlled, draggy maneuvers and that they will lose altitude at the current power setting. Have them return to the wings level crab and repeat this exercise several times, perhaps adding power to maintain altitude, until the student feels comfortable with making the transition from crab to side-slip and back. Repeat the exercise by flying a 180-degree turn, and lining up on the road again so the student has a chance to learn the feel of this maneuver by performing slips in both directions.

This is a very good opportunity to continue into the teaching of forward slips for altitude loss. Show them that if one pushes the rudder too far in a sideslip, it becomes a forward slip, with the nose pointing slightly downwind from the desired flight path. Also point out that the CG of the aircraft is now flying in a direction different than where the nose is pointing. I will cover teaching forward slips during landing approaches later in the section on three point landings.

After this first introduction to the side-slip, it is highly beneficial to a student's training to follow up this exercise with one at the airport, provided you have a runway with some crosswind. For those of you trying to teach at a towered airport you may be able to secure clearance. For those of you at air-carrier airports, your best bet is to find a nearby un-controlled field to use. The exercise is simple.

Make a long approach where your student must use what they have just learned to keep the aircraft aligned with the centerline. However, instead of landing, simply fly down the runway at an altitude of approximately thirty feet while maintaining alignment. Repeat at twenty feet when the student is ready and then again at ten feet if the student is capable. A benefit of this exercise is it removes some of the anxiety most students feel about maneuvering close to the runway and this will help them later when they are learning how to round out into ground-effect during a three-point or wheel landing. Depending on your location and other flight activity, you may be able to reverse direction on the low-pass so your student can deal with crosswind from both sides.

Personally, I try to teach crosswind skills as much as possible. When the wind is within limits, use a crosswind runway even if it is blowing directly down another. Crosswind landing competency is more than just a desirable skill, it is essential to the future well being of your student. By ensuring your students have good crosswind skills, you have a chance to reduce the number of runway loss-of-control accidents that seem to plague us year after year. You will also be giving your students a gift of more flying on windy days while the less skilled sit it out in their hangars.

Judging Height Above Runway

This is one skill important to teaching three point (and wheel) landings not normally addressed separately by instructors. Three-point landings consist of three different pieces of course: the constant airspeed approach glide, the round-out or the process of bringing the descent rate to zero, and the flare, where the aircraft is pitched up into a three-point attitude so all three wheels contact the runway simultaneously. Ending a round out too high will cause problems, resulting in the aircraft suddenly dropping, sometimes from a considerable height, onto the runway. Depending on the student's subsequent actions, either the main gear will strike first or the aircraft will be dropped on its tail.

When the nose is not lifted into a three-point attitude during the drop, the mains strike the runway first and then the tail drops, increasing the wing's angle of attack and, with the increased lift, the airplane climbs back into the air. Seeing this 'bounce' back into the air, the student will usually push the stick forward, diving and causing the main gear to strike the runway again, which then causes the tail to slam down, the angle of attack to increase and the process to repeat. At best, the crow hopping diminishes in intensity

34

and the airplane finally stays on the ground. At worst, the student enters a pilot induced oscillation, or PIO, that gets more vigorous with each cycle and ends with a prop strike or loss of control accident. Neither situation is desirable.

If the tail-wheel strikes the runway first when dropping on from a high round-out, the angle of attack will be suddenly reduced as the nose drops, and the main-gear may strike the runway with great force, damaging the aircraft.

Recovery from both nose-high and nose-low situations is possible and I will cover those procedures in the section on three point and wheel landings as the focus on this section is how get the student to place the aircraft in a tenable position above the runway to execute a safe landing.

I teach that maintaining approach speed into the round out is a desirable condition. In fact, I teach my students they can make their approach at almost any speed, provided their landing area is long enough. Of course, this means the student must learn to stop their descent in the round out and wait for the speed to bleed off while gradually pitching up into a three-point attitude as the airplane sinks to the runway.

One of the common problems students experience is not understanding that for a normal approach and landing, the round-out begins approximately a wing span above the runway, ends in ground effect with the main gear about three feet above the runway surface, and at a speed only marginally below the selected approach speed. Most students will suddenly pull back on the stick when beginning their round out and wind up leveling off much too high.

To teach the round out, I fly the student down the runway at a height of about three feet while telling them to *focus on the far end of the runway and to note their pitch attitude*. Then I have the student fly the same maneuver from both shallow and steep approaches until they can consistently bring their descent rate to zero approximately three to five feet from the ground, and continue the low-pass at that height down the length of the runway.

Advise your student during this process that as the descent rate increases with steeper approaches, the height where the round out is begun must increase to allow sufficient time to slow the aircraft's descent rate to zero at the desired height above the runway. To let the student visualize this, ask them to imagine a vertical approach at high speed versus a shallow two or three degree approach.

The low-pass, conducted a few feet above the ground is also excellent reinforcement that the aircraft must be flown one-hundred percent of the time until the engine stops and the airplane is at rest. It is very common for students to get close to the runway in their round-out and then stop flying, believing the aircraft will finish the landing by itself while drifting sideways and weathervaning into a cross-wind.

The Flare

Of the three components to a three-point landing, the flare is perhaps the most difficult to master. Assuming the student has stopped their descent at an appropriate height above the runway, the most common problems during the last few feet of the landing seem to be increasing the pitch beyond three-point as the aircraft settles or, more commonly, not lifting the nose into the three point attitude at all. Both can cause the problems I've described in the chapter on Judging Height Above the Runway.

One technique I use to teach this component of the landing is a low pass down the runway with the landing gear a few feet above the runway surface. You will need to know the power setting required to hold the aircraft off the runway at less than your normal landing speed. In my 85hp Champ, I use 60 mph as the normal no-wind approach speed, and 50-55 mph as the speed of the low-pass. My power setting for this is somewhere between 1900 and 2000 rpm. You may have to experiment a bit to find the right power setting for your given load. It is best if you set up the approach and demonstrate this maneuver first. Then help them with the approach, rounding out and setting power until your student understands what you are asking them to do.

By flying the low-pass at 50-55 mph, the aircraft will be flying in ground effect in a three-point attitude down the runway. Perform this maneuver until the student can keep the aircraft aligned to the centerline, a few feet above the surface, down the length of the runway. Tell them if the wheels touch, to keep on flying the aircraft and you will help them with a workable power setting. From this exercise they will learn a proper three-point pitch attitude, learn that the aircraft must be flown at all times, improve their alignment skills, and improve their fine pitch control.

Now advise them that after they have established their attitude in the low-pass, you will slowly reduce power while they continue to hold the aircraft in the three-point pitch attitude. When the wheels contact the surface, remove all power and have them bring the stick aft and come to a stop. Let them know they have just performed a powered three-point landing. Have them repeat the maneuver, reducing power on their own and coming to a complete stop.

The next step is to have the student perform their approach, round-out and flare with less and less power so the student can see how power affects the time the aircraft will spend in level flight above the runway during the round out before sinking to the surface. Finally, of course, the goal is to remove all power before beginning the round out.

As the last step in teaching three-point landings with this technique, increase the approach speed so the student can see how the extra kinetic energy of the aircraft is converted into a longer period of time in the round-out, the same as if more energy were added to the aircraft by increasing throttle during the round-out.

Another technique for teaching the flare, related to the low speed low pass, is to mark the students horizon with a highly visible round colored sticker while the student sits in the aircraft. You can also use a fine point dry-erase marker and draw a small circle (one inch) on the outside of the windshield as they focus on the horizon. Tell them when they flare to put the circle on the horizon and hold it there with increasing backpressure until the wheels contact the ground and the stick is brought fully back. This technique seems to work for all students, ab initio or not.

It works especially well for tri-cycle gear pilots who have lots of hours flaring their Skyhawk's, Arrow's and Mooney's into a much lower pitch attitude. I believe the horizon-dot method is the most effective way to eliminate the negative transfer of pitch attitude caused by high time in a tri-cycle gear airplane. However, unlike the low speed pass, it does not reinforce the need for alignment or continued manipulation of the controls during the flare. You must bring attention to those two items if necessary when using this technique.

In summary, I favor using the low-speed low-pass for ab-initio students with no prior pitch attitude habits, and the dot-horizon method for already certificated tricycle gear pilots.

While teaching three-point landings, you must ensure the student knows how to recover from unsafe low and high *ballooning,* more commonly, and incorrectly, called bouncing. A balloon occurs during an attempted three-point landing whenever more lift from the wing exists than the loaded weight of the aircraft. This can be caused by the main gear contacting the runway before the tailwheel, a sudden increase in headwind, the student pulling the stick back too far while flaring, or too high a descent rate when attempting a wheel landing (covered in a later chapter). Recovery from the balloon caused by all of these conditions is the same.

In the case where the pilot has not maintained a three-point pitch attitude and the main gear contacts the runway before the tailwheel, the wing's angle of attack increases as the tailwheel descends, thereby increasing the wing's lift, which subsequently results in the aircraft climbing away from the runway surface. Recovery technique depends on how high above the runway the aircraft balloons, and the degree of runway misalignment during the recovery.

In the case where the aircraft only ascends a few feet, simply get the airplane in three-point attitude, aligned with the centerline, and wait for touchdown.

If the aircraft balloons to a height of from three to about ten feet, apply power at the *top* of the balloon, and slow the aircraft's descent to the surface of the runway while maintaining both a three-point pitch attitude and runway alignment. Remove power only after touchdown.

If the balloon is more than about ten feet, perhaps because of a high approach speed or a sudden stiff gust of wind, it is usually better to abort the landing and go around with full power in a climb pitch attitude. The probability of misalignment to the centerline of the runway or weathervaning into the wind towards the side of the runway is pretty high in this situation.

Remember, the techniques for recovering from a balloon are the same whether caused by inappropriate pitch attitudes, twitchy elevator control, or gusty winds.

Wheel Landings

Wheel landings seem to be the boogey men of tailwheel flying. Fraught with warnings of prop-strikes, the student can become overly anxious with the maneuver. This anxiety only increases if you are obligated to provide a warning about who will pay for a new propeller should a prop strike occur.

This area of training must be briefed, briefed and briefed again until the student completely understands that pushing the stick forward without the main gear in contact with the runway surface is a recipe for disaster. However, this alone will not prevent a prop strike. The best approach seems to be warning the student that when *any* balloon occurs during an attempted wheel landing, *the only appropriate responses* are turning the attempt into a three-point landing, or going-around. That advice, coupled with the instructor's hand lightly on the stick and in an attitude of hyper-vigilance, seems to be pretty effective but not fool proof, believe me. I've gone through four props (wood) in the past twenty years.

I demonstrate an acceptable wheel landing while pointing out the low descent rate used. After briefing them on what will happen, I demonstrate a ballooned (bounced) wheel landing with the appropriate recovery to a three-point landing instead. Point out that the balloon is identical to the balloon of a three-point landing when touchdown occurs with the main gear first.

One important point to show them is the effect of increased drag in ground effect. This sudden effect slows the aircraft enough to increase the descent rate for the last few feet to the runway. This most likely will result in the main gear contacting the runway at too high a descent rate, resulting in a ballooned landing. The pilot's defense against this subtle effect is to focus on the end of the runway in order to detect and prevent any tendency for the nose to pitch down.

This is the key to wheel landings for most students: advise them to keep their focus on the end of the runway until the main gear decides to come into contact with the runway. In other words, not to anticipate a wheel touch but to wait until that happens before easing the stick forward slightly and pinning the main gear onto the runway. Focusing on the end of the runway encourages the student to control the pitch attitude in order to preserve the slow descent rate to touchdown. If the student stops trying to slow the descent rate, ideally bringing it to zero as the wheels touch, or allows the subtle effect of ground-effect drag to increase the descent rate, a ballooned landing will likely occur.

When learning this maneuver, it is important that the airspeed not bleed off quickly between round out and touchdown. To this end, once the student has learned to round out low and in ground effect, show them how to gradually bring the power back up to a slightly lower power setting than required for level flight in the pattern at sixty to sixty-five miles per hour. This power setting will result in a slow descent rate when flying in ground effect between fifty-five and sixty miles per hour. It is essential that the focus be kept on the end of the runway to detect pitch change during this process. Eventually, the wheels will gently touch, usually surprising the student. A little assistance with forward stick to pin the main gear down while removing power is appropriate. This will demonstrate how soft the wheel touch can be and that one need not push the stick forward as if fending off a charging rhino.

Learning wheel-landings is normally the most difficult of the tailwheel skills to be mastered. It usually takes students several hours of instruction to even begin to perform them competently. What is critically important is that the student understands and has integrated the recovery techniques into their flying. Mastering wheel-landings in diverse conditions requires practice. Once the student is able to perform three consecutive landings and, even more importantly, is able to recover a botched attempt safely and effectively, they have demonstrated competency in wheel

landings.

Knowing The Airplane

Training in a Champ or a Cub is probably one of the best ways to learn to fly "conventional" gear aircraft. However, the Tailwheel Endorsement we give to students upon completion of their training may entitle them to fly tailwheel airplanes of decidedly different characteristics.

Realize that one type of landing may not be the best choice for a particular aircraft. A P51 Mustang should probably not be wheel landed because of the small prop clearance. In like fashion it should be flown off in three-point to avoid a potential prop strike. C47's should probably never be landed three-point when loaded, especially on rough terrain. Stinson 103's love to wheel land with gear that simply soaks up large descent rates. Luscombs with their narrower stance are a bit more squirrely on directional control. Cessna 120's and 140's require the fine use of brake during heavier crosswinds as there is not enough rudder authority to provide solid directional control.

These comments are not meant to dissuade anyone from flying any of these fine tailwheel aircraft (and so many more which must remain unmentioned). My comments are to remind you that not all tailwheel aircraft will behave the same under the same conditions. The behavior of each one should be explored with caution, preferably with someone expert in that aircraft's behavior.

This brings up a question I am asked by just about every student I've ever had: When should I use a wheel landing?

I then explain that in the Champ, probably the safest type of landing in strong and squirrelly crosswind is a powered three-point and not a full stall three-point or a wheel landing. The aircraft is most vulnerable while slowing to stall speed just above the runway in a three-point landing. A gust can do just about anything to your directional control.

If you instead fly the airplane onto the ground in three-point attitude with power as in a soft field landing, you will increase the effectiveness of your control surfaces with the increased slipstream from the propeller. Depending on the strength of the direct headwind component, one can often use a significant amount of power in the process without increasing the landing distance.

Finally, with a standard wheel landing, there is a period of vulnerability to wind gusts when slowing down to plant the tailwheel. However, you can modify this technique by using judicious amounts of power to increase control surface effectiveness while flying the tailwheel to the runway in the same fashion as with a powered three-point..

So, take your pick between a powered three-point, and a modified (powered) wheel landing for the Champ. My recommendation is a powered three-point because of its simplicity as compared to the modified (powered) wheel landing. And this is not the definitive word, either. The pilot's preference, pilot skill and aircraft characteristics all enter into the decision as to which type of landing might be best under any given situation.

My last advice is to find what works best for you and your aircraft, and then to practice, practice, practice. You'll wind up at Carnegie Hall, guaranteed.

Teaching Strategies

One of the most fundamental teaching techniques for complex functions is decomposition. With this technique, a complex maneuver is broken down into its constituent functions, with each function practiced separately, and sequentially, by the student.

For example, simply flying straight and level requires that rudder input occur simultaneously with both pitch and roll inputs. If a student is wandering all over the sky trying to perform all three at the same time, make it easier for them; remove a flight control—or two.

First, take the stick and hold pitch and roll constant while they concentrate on yaw and the necessary rudder inputs to pin the nose on a spot directly ahead in the distance. Within a short period of time their rudder inputs will begin to become automatic and the yawing will decrease.

The next step is where you yourself control the rudders while the student controls the pitch and roll of the aircraft. Most students will be able to do this without a lot of difficulty but it will take a bit longer to integrate both pitch and roll than for yaw.

Finally, when the student has convinced themselves they can perform either exercise separately, give them back both stick and rudders. Initially, they will wander around a bit but quickly learn to use all the controls simultaneously to achieve straight and level flight.

Another example might be teaching a student the seat-of-the-pants feel for co-ordination. You hold the bank constant in a turn while you co-ordinate with rudder. Point out the slip/skid ball's position in the center and have them notice how their weight feels straight up and down relative to their seat.

Now skid the aircraft with too much rudder and ask the student which way they are sliding on their seat. When they can feel the sliding motion to the outside of the turn, show them a slip and again ask which way they are sliding in their seats.

Keep the aircraft in the turn and have them try to center their weight with the rudder, coaching them during the process. Once they have accomplished this in left turns, for example, reverse and have them try in turns to the right.

Both the straight-and-level example and the seat-of-the-pants example illustrate the process of deconstruction and how to use it to help your students.

Continue to use all of the other methods you are familiar with. Demonstrate a maneuver, coach them through the same maneuver while providing assistance, and finally simply coaching them while they perform the maneuver by themselves usually works pretty well. If, after repeated attempts, the student is still unable to perform the desired maneuver, you need to stop and tell yourself to take another approach. Repeated head bashing will not change the outcome.

This is when you need to be highly analytical in identifying the reason why the maneuver is not being performed correctly. Once you are sure of your analysis, then you will be able to formulate an adaptive response to that problem. At this point, deconstruction may be used to create an exercise or action to correct the fundamental problem.

An example: Your student cannot control airspeed in level flight to within +/- 10 mph.

Analysis: Student is grossly over-controlling pitch because of a death grip on the neck of the serpent-stick in front of them or is paying no attention to their level flight pitch reference.

Response 1: You trim aircraft to hands off, then have student grasp stick with only their thumb and index finger while resting their forearm on their knee.

Response 2: You trim aircraft to hands off, have student mark horizon with large dot on windshield with a dry erase marker, then have them hold the dot on the horizon with only thumb and index finger on stick.

I don't believe there is any aspect of flight control that cannot be addressed by application of decomposition. However, when a maneuver has been decomposed into its fundamental components and the student is unable to perform, after repeated attempts, one of those components, you must think through the potential causes for that lack of success and act accordingly. Student fatigue, illness, physical inability, lack of sleep, and stress in personal life are all possible explanations. You must tread carefully here, asking leading questions in an attempt to uncover the fundamental problem without being overly intrusive. It is critical for you to develop an open, honest and trusting style of communication with your student.

If, despite your best efforts at correcting some aspect of your student's performance, no progress is being made, it is time for another instructor to ride along with your student. Discuss the student's problem with the other instructor and ask them to both confirm your analysis (e.g., not enough pitch control), and attempt to correct that problem with an appropriate exercise (e.g., pitch up/down to five mph/knot airspeed increments).

The other instructor may notice something you've missed, or may devise an approach you have not tried which seems to work. If this is what happens, then your student is off and running again, making progress in their training.

But if, despite the other instructor's best (perhaps multiple) attempts to correct the student's problem no progress is made, it is probably time to have a heart-to-heart discussion on the future of their training. They should understand exactly what the problem is, why mastering that maneuver is important to flight, and that you have exhausted your bag of tricks in an attempt to help them learn the maneuver.

Let them know you are willing to keep trying until hell freezes over if necessary, but they will eventually have to demonstrate competence in the maneuver to earn their pilot's certificate.

Your student must understand their options: it will take more time (read money) than anticipated for them to reach their goal, you are willing to continue with them if they are willing, and that you are also prepared to find them another instructor if they prefer.

I know this sounds like admitting defeat with the student and, in many ways, you are. After all, despite your best efforts you have not been able to teach that student some essential skill required for flight. But you have probably taught them many other things about flying along the way, and there may be reasons beyond your control you are not even aware of. A death, divorce, or loss of a beloved pet can all cause immense grief and stress, all of which is reflected in your student's state of mind when they climb into the aircraft. A toxic home environment can have unpredictable effects on the student's performance, as can high levels of stress. I once had a young woman burst into tears after multiple attempts at landing with a 7-8 knot crosswind. After I took the controls she blurted, "My mom has cancer." Keep in mind at all times that your student, despite appearances, male, female, young, old, large or small, are all human beings trying to get through each day as best they can; just like you.

In our next chapter we're going to look at how some of the different personality characteristics play out during flight instruction and how you must be able to recognize and deal with them to make progress with your student.

Unusual Attitudes

To help assess how best to teach your student, and to advise you of some of the personality issues that may arise, the FAA has promulgated a list of five "Hazardous Attitudes" for you to be watchful for during instruction[3]. They are: Resignation, Anti-authority, Impulsivity, Invulnerability and Macho".

The problem with such a list is that without further training in psychological evaluation, slapping one of these labels on your student is bound to be only partially accurate, at best. Instead of trying to pick our way through this minefield, I want to discuss two situations that I deal with continuously: anxiety and perfectionism.

The primary emotion in learning to fly, underlying any 'affect' or presented attitude or action, is anxiety. It would be the rare individual indeed who, truth be known, does not climb into that cockpit the first time full of

---

[3] "Pilot's Handbook of Aeronautical Knowledge." Pilot's Handbook of Aeronautical Knowledge. Accessed June 28, 2016.
http://www.faa.gov/regulations_policies/handbooks_manuals/aviation/pilot_handbook/.

anxiety, with a racing pulse and elevated blood pressure, caused by what they are thinking about the process.

This anxiety must be addressed the first time you meet your student. Probably uppermost in their mind at this point is how their relationship with you is going to work. Anxiety about the actual process of learning to fly is a close second. The first few minutes of your conversation will allow you to set the tone for all future instruction and show them your primary focus is on the way they learn best. Advise them that all students are anxious to one degree or another, and they should communicate that anxiety to you as you work through their flight training. This alone will go a long way toward establishing that your number one objective is effectively transferring your knowledge of flying to them during training.

Let your students know anxiety is normal, and provide them an opportunity to acknowledge that anxiety which is the first step towards reducing its impact on the learning process.

External signs of anxiety can take many forms depending on how the individual has learned to respond to high stress situations: Machine gun speech, jerky movement, clammy skin, rapid eye movement, short attention span, fixation, etc.

Most students will honestly admit to feeling some anxiety if asked. If you tell them "Most students feel some anxiety about learning to fly," you will give them permission to express that anxiety openly.

However, if your student outwardly exhibits some swaggering bravado about learning to fly, they most likely are unable to acknowledge their anxiety. But the first time they become overwhelmed with external stimulae, fixate, and ignore your voice over the intercom, don't be surprised.

Fortunately, the approach to dealing with student anxiety for both those willing to acknowledge it, and those who would never admit such a thing, is the same: gradual, repeated exposure, and clear explanations of what to expect. This is where the importance of a pre-flight briefing can be invaluable by telling them in advance what they might see and feel during the lesson, thereby removing much anxiety about the unknown.

A good example of a student bringing some preconceived attitude into the process is what they think or have been told about stalls. A bit of calm, reasoned explanation about learning this process before your first lesson on stalls will go a long way toward pulling the fangs of this dragon.

Occasionally, you may have a student who is simply overwhelmed by the beauty and majesty of it all, and they will ignore your repeated questions the same as if fixated by anxiety. This may be a loss of situational awareness at some level, but I tend to think the student's ability to process new sensory information is simply overloaded.

If you can get the student through the first lesson of straight and level, some gentle turns, climbs and descents, much of their anxiety will quickly disappear.

The biggest area of anxiety for most students (if not instructors) is power-on stalls. Depending on the aircraft you are flying, the deck angles can become very steep before the actual stall occurs. Combining a high deck angle with a lot of engine noise, sloppy controls and the specter of a potential spin, is a sure recipe for student anxiety. This is an area you need to approach carefully with your student, but you can only do so if you are totally comfortable with both power-on stalls, incipient spins and spin recovery.

The FAA requires sixty-five percent power or more to be used in the demonstration of power-on stalls[4]. Use your POH or engine manual to determine the power setting required for your aircraft. Now you know the *minimum* power setting the examiner will accept. I begin teaching power-on stalls at pattern altitude power settings and airspeed. In my 85HP Champ, that translates to approximately 2000 rpm at sixty to sixty-five miles per hour, depending upon load.

Beginning your power-on stall training at a low power setting permits you to ease the student into gradually more dramatic deck angles and noise levels, giving you the chance to stress co-ordination and the effects of slow flight on aircraft handling. Adopting a gradual approach will go a long way towards reducing the anxiety associated with this maneuver.

Let me reiterate the importance of briefing the student on the maneuvers to be performed during the lesson, discussing what sensations

---

4 "Airman Certification Standards." Airman Certification Standards. Accessed June 28, 2016. http://www.faa.gov/training_testing/testing/acs/.

they may experience during the process, and answering any of their questions. This is the best time to inoculate your students against unreasonable anxiety.

Another attitude I want to talk about is *unreasonable* perfectionism or perhaps better said, unreasonable expectations. There is nothing wrong about striving for perfection, and if you hope to become a better, safer pilot over time, you must have some desire to improve your skills. An attitude of *unreasonable* expectations, however, like Lucifer perched on your shoulder, whispers in your ear after just a few attempts, you *should* be able to master the maneuver, especially if it is seemingly simple, like flying turns around a point.

If this sub-conscious advice is allowed to prevail, the student's conclusion can be as judgmental as deciding they are not cutout for flight training. This unwarranted attitude is as much an obstacle to flight training as blindness. And, in a way, it is a psychological blindness which prevents these students from allowing themselves the freedom, and necessity, to make mistakes during the learning process.

Sometimes, students are rewarded with acceptable performance on their first few attempts at a new maneuver. As all instructors are aware, this simply means they got lucky and, when the student is asked to perform the maneuver again, perhaps under slightly different conditions, the results are vastly different. However, to the student with unreasonable expectations of performance, this is an unacceptable failure.

The only approach I have found that seems to have any effect at all is to let this type of student know upfront, that some of the things they learn will come easy, some with moderate effort, and some only with fairly extensive practice, like a good cross-wind wheel landing, and that Mother Nature cares not about IQ, prior technical knowledge in another field or the number of advanced degrees hanging on the walls of their office. Successful people in other fields of endeavor seem to be especially vulnerable to a type of thinking which demands they excel at flying the same as they excel at medicine, or computer programming. Some may, some may not.

Learning to fly an aircraft is more than an intellectual activity, requiring not only hand-eye co-ordination and sound judgment, but also a willingness to be wrong while learning. It requires a student's acceptance of stumbling through mistakes while being coached and protected until a new skill is mastered. This is the job of the flight instructor, and you can help this process by letting them know they were not born with wings, and that flying an aircraft is unlike anything they have done before in their lives. Let them know you expect them to fail, time after time, during the learning process. It is your job to help them learn from those mistakes and eventually to master the new skill.

Students will often ask how they are coming along compared to average student progress. I usually tell them there is no such thing as an average except in mathematical terms and even then, the number is virtually meaningless except from a high-level, macro, point of view.

I've read somewhere the average flight times for a Private Pilot certificate are over seventy hours now. How can anyone apply that statistic, with any degree of accuracy, to an individual student who ranges in age from eighteen to seventy, or for those with the hand-eye coordination of a tennis pro, or to someone who was their class's favorite target in fifth grade dodge ball? We all learn at different rates, and with different degrees of retention. My experience leads me to believe that the factors that affect learning the most are: age, intelligence, attitude, frequency of lessons and some prior science education.

Age is kind of a loaded factor, I believe. Simple life experience that comes with age can enhance the learning process but youthful hand-eye co-ordination can often make precise maneuvering easily learned. I am not aware of any studies that have examined the effect of age on flight training. To do so would require that the other variables of intelligence, attitude and lesson frequency be controlled. We run into the same problem when attempting to isolate any one of the aforementioned factors and its effect on speed of learning.

In addition to the difficulty in holding (or adjusting) lesson frequency to remove its effect while attempting to study the age variable, how would you normalize intelligence and attitude? Not many people have taken any kind of standardized IQ test, and what acceptably common scale could we possibly use to measure attitude? These are just some of the difficulties in answering questions about how long it should take someone to earn a particular rating and I would suggest you emphasize the highly individualized process it really is when you have this discussion with your student, and particularly when your student is trying to get a handle on the financial commitment they will be making.

Reports of average hours for the Private Pilot certificate by operators of Part 141 flight schools or other flight schools offering accelerated training must be placed in an appropriate context. Their students are almost invariably quite young, with adequate funds and an intense desire to pursue aviation as a vocation. This demographic is vastly different than the forty-five to fifty year old whose children have now finished college, leaving them with the funds and time to pursue a lifelong interest.

As I have attempted to stress throughout this work, everyone learns a bit differently, and your teaching methods need to adapt themselves to best serve your student.

FINAL THOUGHTS

I hope that as an instructor, you find some inspiration within these pages that will help you teach tailwheel flying effectively. However, no technique is an all-purpose panacea for student problems and there is certainly room for experimentation and new techniques.

I also hope that I have adequately described the process of task deconstruction. This process will enable you to devise your own personalized methods of teaching for those students who just can't seem to get it and need a different approach. Try thinking out of the box: there may be psychological factors affecting a student's inability to round out without ballooning for example. The real problem may be fear of slamming the gear into the runway, or something they may have heard about prop strikes.

Ultimately, your job as an instructor is to make sure your students thoroughly understand what you are teaching, and are able to demonstrate that knowledge to your satisfaction. I think there are few other teaching jobs that are as personal or as intellectually and physically demanding, as flight instruction.

I cherish the personal relationships I have made over the years with all of my students and I want to formally thank each and every one of them for their contributions to my store of knowledge. Unknowingly, each has left some small legacy for those who later came to fly with me and without them this book would not exist.

Never stop trying to become better at your craft than you currently are. Give one hundred plus percent to your students, and be proud of what you can do for them. To steal a title from one of my favorite authors, Richard Bach, I think it almost spiritual and intensely rewarding to be able to give The Gift of Wings. I hope you learn to feel the same.

End

Made in the USA
Las Vegas, NV
09 May 2021